MY FARM

Alison Lester

to Mum and Dad, for a wonderful childhood

A
LITTLE
ARK
BOOK

ALLEN & UNWIN

When I was little I lived on a farm overlooking the sea.
Through summer, autumn, winter, and spring we worked on the land together,

Mum,   Dad,   Charlie,   Kate,   Jake,   and me.

We rode our horses every day and loved them like friends.

The year my old pony died, Charlie let me ride his horse while he used the motor bike. Tricky was all right, but I really missed Inky.

In summer we checked the water troughs to make sure the thirsty cattle had enough to drink. Sometimes we drove the old jinker and stopped for a swim along the way.

We shifted mobs of cattle to better pasture and sorted out some that were ready to sell.

On market days huge trucks backed up to the dusty stockyards. Dogs barked, bullocks bellowed, whips cracked, and we yelled 'Oi! Oi! Oi!', 'Get up!', and 'Hooooah!' to drive the cattle up the ramp.

One moonlit night a truck arrived with some new cows. I went up to the yards with my father to unload them. Something spooked the cattle, and in a flash they were racing down the road. I chased them on Tricky, riding bareback in my pyjamas, and finally brought them home.

I felt like a real hero.

Late in summer, bushfires sometimes broke out in the hills. The smoke cast an eerie yellow light over our farm. We kept a water tank on the truck in case one of the paddocks caught fire.

Blackberries were ripe for picking then, and the apples in the orchard were crunchy and delicious.

The local show was always a big day for us. It took weeks to get ready. We washed the stud bulls and cows, and taught them how to parade.

We brushed our ponies until they shone, and plaited their manes and tails. Dad taught Tricky to jump.

Jake practised his tricks on Bella…

…and trained Sadie for the dog high-jump.

My best friend Maggie double-dinked with me,
and we won the Quietest Pony Contest.
But Charlie took the ribbon because Tricky
was his horse.

I really wished I had my own pony.

Dad's bull was the Grand Champion that year,
and Sadie came third in the dog high-jump.

In autumn the trees turned orange and red. We galloped through the fallen leaves, sending them spinning behind us.

New cattle arrived from the Snowy Mountains, and Dad and Uncle Jack drove them down the beach to spend winter on the bush run.

When the cows began to calve we had to check them at least twice a day.

Once I found an abandoned calf, and carried him home on Tricky. Mum made a bed for the shivering baby in front of the stove, and I fed him warm milk from a bottle. He sucked my fingers with his raspy tongue.

Sometimes a calf died, and we had to find a new baby for its mother.

Dad bought an orphan calf from our neighbour, and dressed it in a jacket made from the dead calf's skin. The cow recognised the smell of her own calf, and adopted the orphan.

If a cow needed help to give birth, we'd drive her slowly to the yards.
Mum delivered the calf, just like a doctor delivering a baby.

I was the assistant, patting the cow and soothing her with my voice.
Sometimes I felt frightened, but it was always thrilling to see
the tiny newborn calf.

After the first autumn rains, mushrooms popped up in the paddocks. We would trudge for miles, with knives and buckets, searching for a whopper or a perfect fairy ring.

We drove the cattle to the yards again, to be dipped and drenched. The mud was as sticky as glue. Once Kate got so stuck she came right out of her boots.

We didn't need to buy much meat from the butcher because we had our own. None of us liked to be around when Dad killed a sheep, but we all loved to help with the cutting-up. We punched off the skin and investigated the insides. The dogs and cats waited for titbits.

On frosty mornings the mist crept into the valleys, and I'd pretend we lived on a Norwegian fiord.

When rainstorms flooded the flat country, Jake and I loved racing through the water. I always got splattered with mud because Tricky was so slow. I thought about the quicksilver pony I'd like to have.

By the time we reached home we had such cold hands Mum had to unbuckle our bridles.

We fed out hay in the cold winter months when the paddocks were bare. The cattle ran after the truck, bellowing for food.

If the grass was very slippery we'd hold onto baling twine and waterski behind the truck.

We plaited the used twine into long skipping ropes.

Even in winter we all had jobs to do.
Jake fed the dogs every day.

Kate milked the house cow. We called her Bambi,
because she was so gentle.

I fed Bambi's calf, and looked after the chooks.

And Charlie looked after the baby wombat Dad had rescued from the side of the road. He was tiny and hairless, and lived in a woollen beanie beside the stove.

Mum found some duck's eggs, and we kept them warm in the electric frying pan until they hatched.

The ducklings thought Mum was their mother.

One of my favourite times was when we had a pioneer settlement down at the creek. Bambi came with us, and we made a yard for her and the ponies.

We built a hut and dammed the creek, hoping to flood the road so we wouldn't have to go to school the next day.

In springtime the ground dried out and we were allowed to ride on the lawn again.

Our best trick was galloping under the clothesline
and grabbing onto it, like cowboys.

Bella was so quiet we could dress her up.

One day Jake rode her into the kitchen, and she left tiny hoofprints on the lino.

Native Australian Zebra

Maggie and I wanted to be famous. We painted clay stripes on the old black horse, so people would think he was a rare type of zebra.

When we went on tadpoling and fishing expeditions the cats, dogs, and our pet sheep all tagged along.

In September it was time to bring the cattle home from the bush run. That year, Jake and I were finally old enough to go along.

It took a day to ride down and muster, and a day to drive them home along the beach. We splashed through the shallows and jumped the waves.

I decided to be a drover when I grew up.

The sweet spring grass was cut into hay, and stored in the sheds to be used next winter.

Mum gave us afternoon tea to take down to the hay carters.

We'd race home across the mown grass, and Kate's pony, Possum, always took off.

My birthday came and went, but I didn't get the pony I'd been hoping for.

After a day's work we cooled down under the sprinkler, or swam our ponies in the dam.

Sometimes we went to the beach and ate our dinner near the soft purple sea.

Charlie was always the boss of our games. He could hypnotise chooks, and sometimes had a whole line of them with their feet in the air. We had to pay to watch this performance. My payment was promising to barrack for Collingwood.

Charlie's dog Sadie had her pups in a hollow log behind the shed.

Our cousins always came for Christmas, and we loved having such a gang.

We played crazy, complicated games, like tightrope-walking, snail races, cat-in-trousers contests …

… building cubbies, and Olympic Games.

When I woke that Christmas there were no presents at the foot of my bed. I searched my pillowcase, but all I found was a slip of paper with the words 'Look in the orchard'.

There under the apple tree was a pony.
A palomino pony.
My own pony.

No one wore safety helmets when I was little, so that's how
I've drawn it, but these days you'd be crazy to ride
without a helmet. So remember, always wear your hard hat,
and ride safely!

A Little Ark Book
First published 1992
Allen & Unwin Pty Ltd
9 Atchison Street, St Leonards, NSW 2065, Australia

National Library of Australia
Cataloguing-in-Publication entry:

Lester, Alison.
My farm.

ISBN 1 86373 374 4

1. Farms - Australia - Juvenile literature.
2. Seasons - Australia - Juvenile literature.
I. Title.

630.994

Set in Berkeley Book by Pixel Pty Ltd, Melbourne
Printed in Australia by Impact Printing